# THE COMPLETE
# HEATH

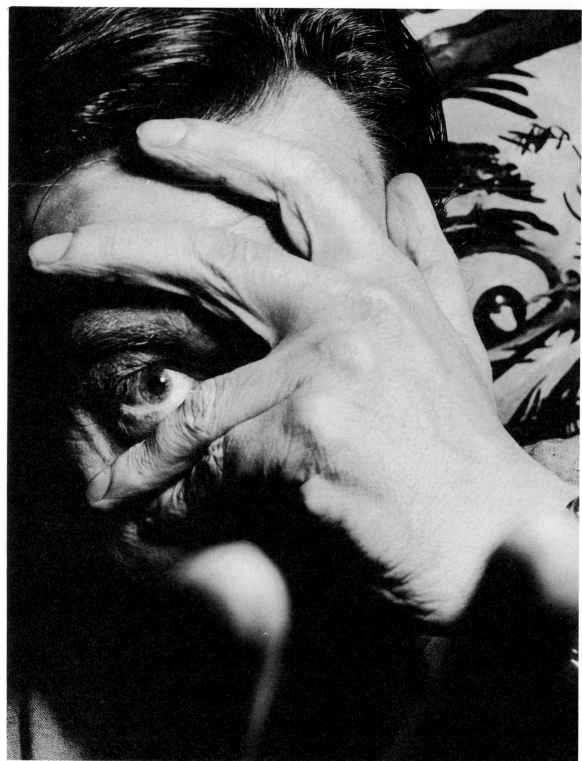

# THE COMPLETE HEATH

A collection of the very best of his
cartoons and strips taken from
*Private Eye, The Spectator, The
Sunday Times* and *The Independent.*

# Michael Heath

John Murray

*In memory of Michael Ffolkes*

© Michael Heath

First published in 1990
by John Murray (Publishers) Ltd
50 Albermarle Street, London W1X 4BD

Photoset by Rowland Phototypesetting Ltd
Bury St Edmunds, Suffolk
Printed in Great Britain by
Butler & Tanner Ltd,
Frome and London

# Contents

# THE SUITS

from *The Spectator*

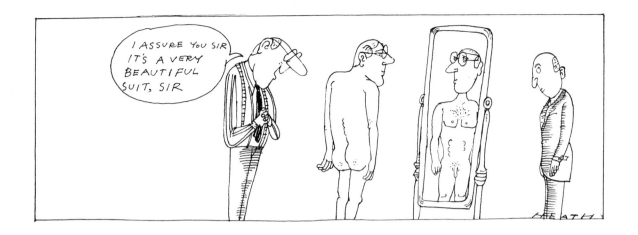

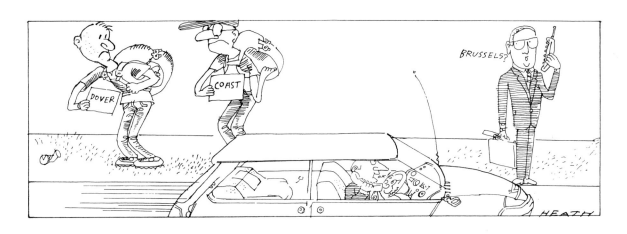

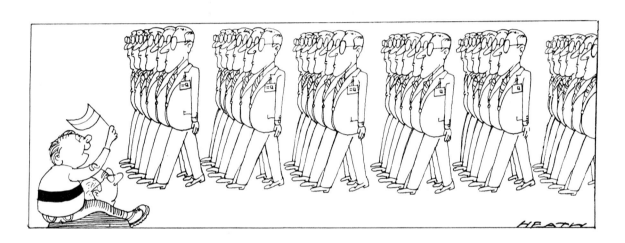

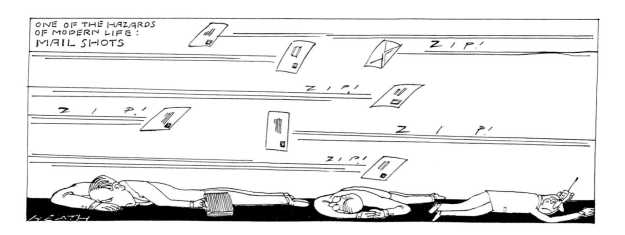

# THE REGULARS

The Regulars are a series of strips that appear in
*Private Eye,* based on the life of Jeffrey Bernard and
other regulars of The Coach and Horses pub in Soho.
These cartoons feature on the set of the hugely
successful West End play *Jeffrey Bernard is Unwell*.

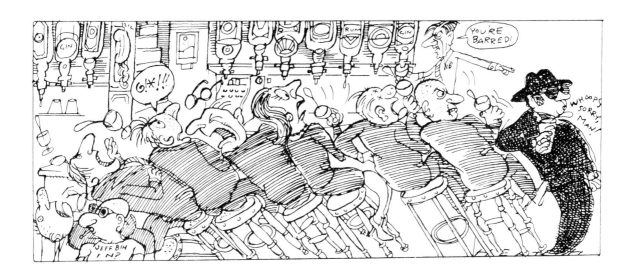

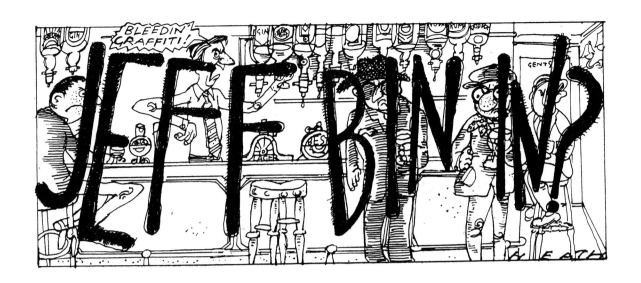

# STYLE VICTIMS

from *The Sunday Times*

'Which one's Kevin?'

'He overdid the studs.'

'No the coat's real,
she's the fake.'

'What is a style victim?'

'Oh, mother! Don't be such a bore!
It's what everybody is wearing!'

'I find that flicking through this once a month keeps me fit.'

'Great. The beehive is back!'

'It's amazing when you consider
he's virtually illiterate.'

''Ere! You're standin' on me hat!'

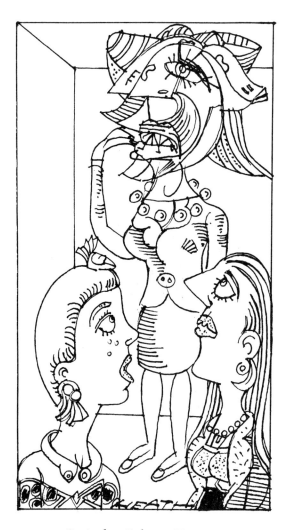

'Isn't that Paloma Picasso?'

'And please bring the hem line down.'

'Super darling, a Barbour nappy!'

'And this I think is my son.'

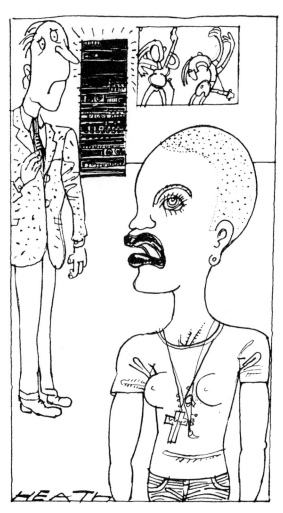

'Don't worry! It's only a wig.'

# NUMERO UNO

from *Private Eye*

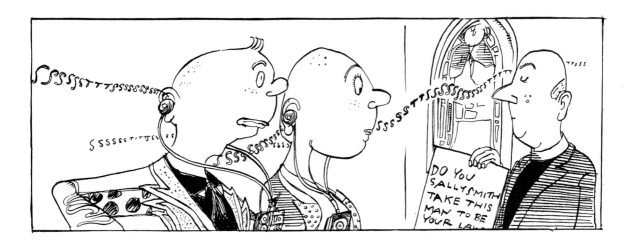

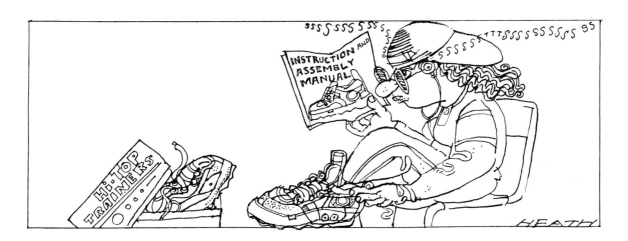

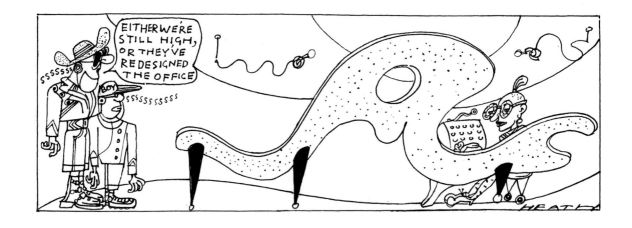

# GREAT BORES
# OF TODAY

from *Private Eye*

with words thanks to
Ian Hislop, Barry Fantoni and Richard Ingrams

"... have you seen the exhibition? it's stunning there are all his
sketchbooks going back you know years and years the output is
absolutely phenomenal all those drawing do you realise he did at least
100 of them a day for 50 years what a genius every one of them is a
masterpiece the sheer energy of the man it takes your breath away the
virtuosity is truly astonishing some are sort of abstract and others are
more realistic but he was so prolific and there they are on show for the
first time one can't take it all in on one visit so we're going again and
we've ordered the book and we've bought a T-shirt for Julian . . ."

"... when you think of modern day technology and all the computers it just seems incredible to me that our Metmen can't predict something like that I mean the French knew hours in advance and so did the Dutch and even Granddad who has a barometer that must have been made in 1890 says it dropped like a stone and it was obvious that something big was on the way he rang me up just think how lucky we were then just the greenhouse and the fence the people down the road had a tree through the bedroom window and the chimneys went right through the roof they were very nearly killed it's so sad to think about all those trees all those lovely trees it just makes you realise how vulnerable we all are for all our sophisticated scientific progress we're still at the mercy of the elements your father slept through it all of course ..."

". . . we decided not to go abroad I mean why have all that hassle at Gatwick and so forth? and by the time you get back you need another holiday we rented this little cottage in Norfolk for two weeks and even though it rained all the time you don't really notice it in Norfolk and there are all these incredible churches and houses which no one ever goes to and because you know we live in this country we're almost blind to it I don't suppose French people ever go to Chartres Cathedral or Versailles we went to these gardens which belonged to that women who wrote the novels and it was amazing nobody there at all we had the place to ourselves and then we found this resturant which was just as good as anywhere in Europe good simple cooking by this lovely couple I expect next year we'll go to Spain again only because the children love the sun so much if it was up to us of course . . ."

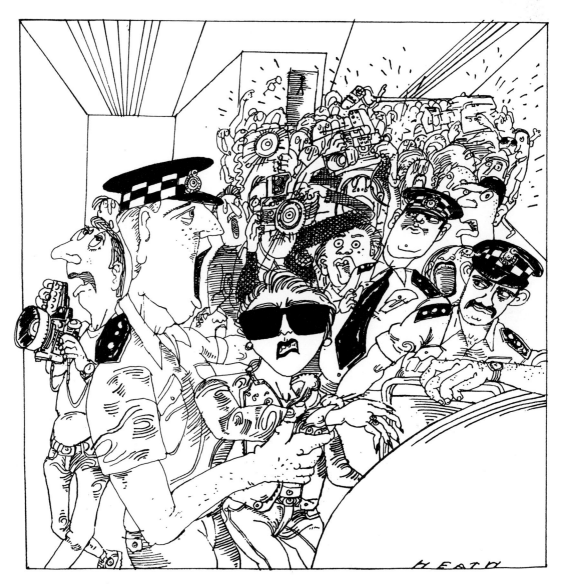

"... she won't last it's all hype no one will remember her in ten years
unlike you know ... I mean he really was the greatest I remember the day he
died I was tiling the bathroom and it came over the radio my wife shouted
out to me 'He's dead' and I knew exactly who she meant and I couldn't take
it in I put on *Love Me Tender* and kept playing it over and over again the
doctor had to put her on pills we went to Gracelands last year for the first
time and the atmosphere was incredible he really was there we saw his suits
hanging up and everything I broke down you know ten years later and his
record sales still outstrip anyone else and he's the only rock star ever to have
topped the country and western and rock charts simultaneously it's
unimaginable when you think about it if I'd had a son I would have called
him Elvis ..."

"... I think it's terrible the way they're being treated what was it at Luton? 3,000 people sleeping on the floor kids and all these friends of ours only booked for a week in Corfu arrived there Saturday morning told there would be a delay 24 hours later they're still sitting there no one tells them anything they put them on the plane and then they take them off again all they gave them was one sandwich in three days they worked out that even if they went by the time they got there they'd have to come back so they went home and you notice it only happens in the summer say what you like about the weather over here at least you don't have to wait a week to get there mind you if you come off the M4 too soon on the way to Devon you'll find you're on a 12-mile tailback to Bristol I think it's terrible ..."

"... I've junked my CD now I had the lot of the range but for jazz forgot it I mean there's no feel to it technically it's magnificent but so what? you lose all the atmosphere I like to have a cardboard album cover in my hand with proper liner notes that you can read without a magnifying glass those early Bluenote US import covers designed by David Stone Martin I mean they are works of art in their own right who cares if there are a few scratches here and there? it's all part of the experience I mean my first record was an old 78 played on a windup I can remember now coming back from the shop with just a plain brown wrapper it was Bunk and George Lewis *Careless Love Blues* I could whistle you the clarinet solo now Dum Dum Dum Dum magic you don't get that on a CD .. "

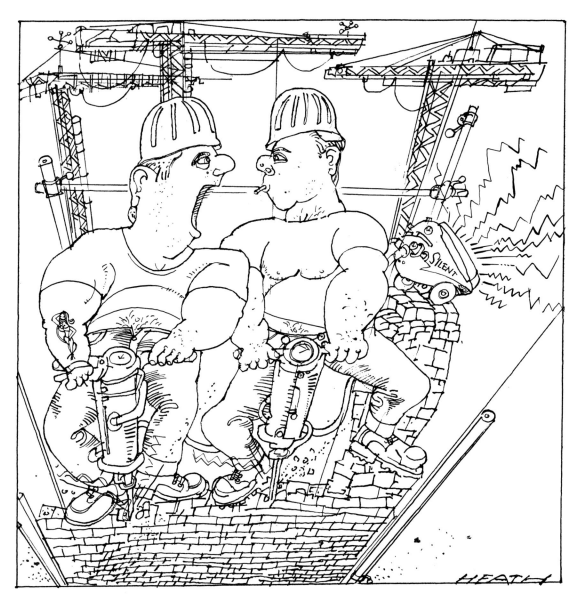

". . . don't talk to me about students they've got it made lying around all day with their drugs and their birds I mean who's paying for them? *we* are you see what they done now? they've elected that darkie who murdered all those blokes with the machete they should take away all their grants and make 'em work for a living like the rest of us they're all wasting time studying some rubbish and what about the relatives? they didn't think about them going round electing murderers they're not kids no matter what they say when I was 18 I was working wasn't I? not sucking up to some convict they're all communists stirred up by the extremists I ask you what are they learning if all they can do is elect a loony? I think Maggie should step in . . . she's marvellous they'd have to listen to her . . ."

"... I think there is room for a new Sunday they've spotted a gap in the market it's got to be a quality one with good writing free from interference and no political bias which will examine issues on their merits alone that's where the others have patently fallen down all that satellite TV and that Harrods stuff and I hate all those sections who needs all that? what we need is a compact appraisal of the week's news really good articles with top quality writing and those mags are a waste of time all full of adverts you don't look forward to the Sundays any more I read the Saturdays now there's plenty in them to take you through to Monday lots of good writing there I mean if you ask me anyone who starts a Sunday needs their head examined ..."

"... what kind of example is that to set to youngsters? effing and blinding in front of the cameras and behaving like a real yob? I mean can you imagine someone like Len Hutton assaulting fellow passengers on the aeroplane or taking drugs? I've got no time for him as for this elephant business obviously it's just a publicity stunt mind you he'll raise a lot of money for leukaemia research and whatever you say about him he's head and shoulders above the rest of that lot cricket always had its larger-than-life characters and I mean if he occasionally goes over the top that's the pressure of media I mean if it wasn't for the papers we wouldn't have heard anything about it I think they should leave him alone it's his wife I feel sorry for ..."

". . . I've never felt better the business is going really well and one thing
I've learnt is that if you want something done you do it yourself we've been
fed all this crap for years about how we can't live without the bastards and
you *can* believe me the sense of freedom is overwhelming you're your own
boss you don't answer to anyone it's basically a question of asserting yourself
and not feeling guilty just because you've acted *for* yourself they've always
been selfish and aggressive we're more self-reliant more able to cope you
know anyway being free doesn't come for nothing but let me tell you the
rewards are well worth it in the work situation the home situation and in the
sack situation you can pick and choose call the shots and not be emotionally
damaged by it I've never felt better it's marvellous really marvellous
really . . ."

"... if he doesn't know you he'll go for you don't matter who you are we had this bloke outside just looking at my car and he was down the garden like a streak of lightning over the gate and 'ad 'im 16 stitches in his leg lucky I was there he'd have killed him coloured kiddie as it happens it's the killer instinct bred in them they use them in the South African police apparently I 'ad an alsatian before he was exactly the same anyone coming to the house he'd never seen he'd be at their throats but with my kids it's amazing they can do what they like little Karen she rides him around like a horse and he don't do nothing he's a real softy they pull his tail and everything you wouldn't believe that he has four tons of pressure in his jaw when he bites they're killers really 'e's in the back of the van now if you want to look at 'im ..."

". . . I think you can feel the change already I think it's going to be a new age less materialism I mean we're going to see an end to all those Porsches and Filofaxes who talks about yuppies anymore? no it's all about spiritual values and saving the planet now we're all responsible for each other the me-decade is over it's an us scenario from now on we have got to take a step into a new dawn it's not just green issues it's not just rediscovering the inner self it's er . . . we've got to stop raiding the planet yes but we've got to redefine ourselves as citizens of the world I mean we're ten years away from the end of the century if you think of the whole of history as 24 hours then mankind has destroyed the earth in 30 seconds even less probably TV was terrible over Christmas wasn't it . . ."

". . . let's face it the Chunnel's going to make all the difference and 1992 is just around the corner and this initiative is just what the country needs we've been an island far too long I'm in rotary mowers myself and I employ 27 people and we're hoping to expand but there's no way without getting into Europe we're talking grass there you've got to keep an eye on the future we're talking 800 million units and that's not peanuts I mean Bruce Oldfield's got the right idea we've got to grasp the nettle and adapt which is the whole point so that our mowers will work in Sweden Athens Salzburg and when Turkey comes in we're talking a bonanza for people like me who've seen the green light and gone for it . . ."

". . . we've stopped buying them it's not that they're not any good some of them are great but there's a limit to how much you can read on a Sunday it's bad enough with all these extra supplements on a Saturday we used to take them all I used to like a nice lie-in with the Sunday papers you could handle them but now I mean you need a wheelbarrow to get them into the house you don't know where to start all those different sections and supplements and the free offers it's overkill you can't take it all in we stopped taking them a fortnight ago and it's just amazing the things you find you can do on a Sunday you've got the whole day to yourself last Sunday I watched all the films on BBC2 and even that *Songs of Praise* is really interesting . . ."

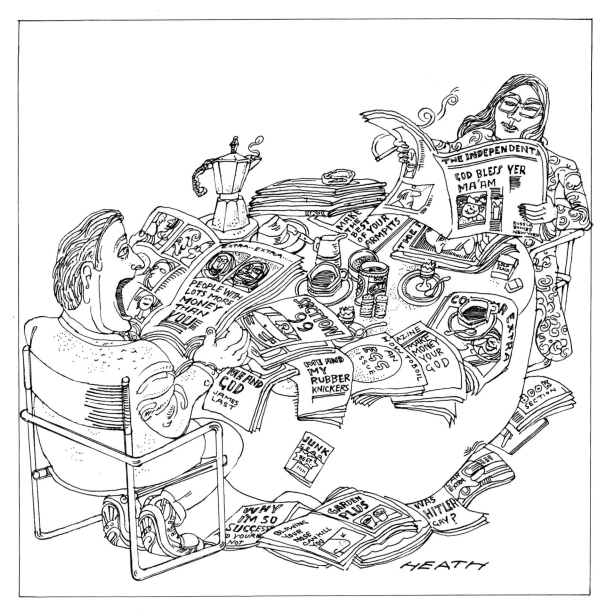

" . . . I mean when you think what man has done to the rain forests in Brazil they're cutting them down at a rate of a thousand acres a day and that means that all this carbon is going up in the atmosphere so we're heating up all the time and this will melt the polar ice caps and this is going to raise the water level worldwide by one and a half metres and that means the whole of New York and London will be under water it's not the bomb we've got to worry about it's Planet Earth and what homo sapiens is doing to it I wake up at night sometimes thinking about that I mean we've only got one planet and there's a limit to what you can plunder even the royal family's got the message I agree with Prince Charles . . ."

". . . no that's the trouble with young people today they've got so much money they don't know what to do with it I mean when we were kids we had to work for it I had a milk round and a paper round and I had to get up at 4.30 in the morning and it really teaches you the value of money that sort of thing kids nowadays expect to be given it on a plate £20–£30 a week for doing nothing and what do they do with it? they just waste it on one-arm bandits and no wonder there's a drug problem with all that money floating around in my day I had to pay for my keep I could hardly afford to go to the pictures even though it was only 1/9 to go in the stalls at the Regal let's have another . . "

". . . you see over there it's an open society they've got Freedom of Information and all that I mean it's written into the constitution you can find out whatever you like you just go to Washington and look it up now if Mrs Thatcher had been doing what Reagan has been up to we'd never have found out until 100 years later when they opened up the files you see they've got a special prosecutor and judicial committees and what have we got? I'll tell you a lot of stuffed shirt civil servants saying 'no comment' I ask you it's a disgrace still that Fifth Amendment lark seems a bit much you don't have to say anything at all I mean I prefer our system actually . . ."

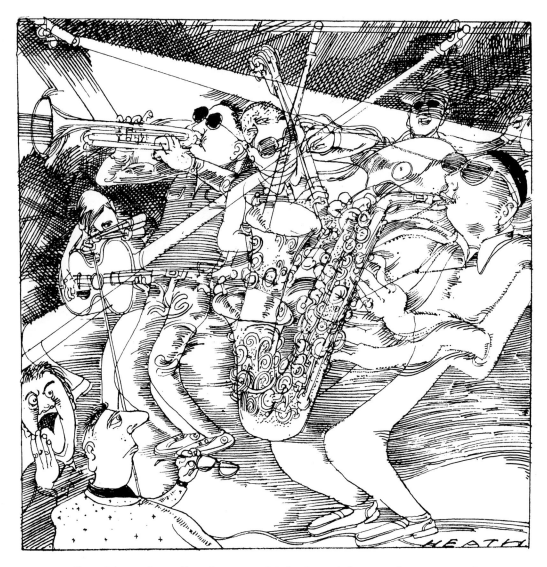

"... it's tragic really when you think about it he was the greatest of his generation his solo on the Miles Davis *Movin'* album back in the Fifties still makes you shiver thousands of players copied him everyone owed something to him no wonder that he turned to drugs when the critics ignored him I mean no one gave him credit when he was discovered last year he was working as a bell hop in Miami they actually had to buy his teeth before he could go back in the studio he's better than ever now Michael Jackson flew him to Toledo just for one riff but my favourite is still that '48 take on Vogue with Lucky Thomson Sonny and Al Haig it's just amazing and he could hardly stand up at the time what a survivor he's coming over soon and he's doing a one nighter at Hove Polytechnic those kids won't know what's hit them ..."

"... they're wasting millions of pounds telling us to be careful when all the facts prove that only one you know straight has actually died from AIDS ever which is staggering you remember all those ads with that girl? well she'd never get it anyway the numbers who've got the virus through normal you know sex are virtually nonexistent here I mean OK New York and Africa may be different I understand that and the exchanging needles and the haemophiliac business obviously distorts the figures but I've got this friend who works in one of the big hospitals and she reckons that the odds of someone like you or me getting it from you know ordinary intercourse are less than being run over by a number 9 bus which proves the point still you've got to be careful cos there was this bloke on the TV last night saying the estimated numbers in ten years' time could top the hundred thousand mark it's terrible could be you and me I'm going for a test on Monday . . ."

"... it's fantastic we go every year and Tuscany is still so unspoilt
and the countryside is absolutely ravishing we rented this little
farmhouse near Siena from my brother-in-law and I must say he's done
it up beautifully you'd hardly know there's a pool in the vineyard and
there's this darling little couple who come in every day and clean up the
leaves and everything and she cooks the most marvellous tagliatelli
with all the herbs that grow wild in the garden you really do get away
from it all we didn't see a soul all the time we were there apart from
Tony Lambton whose villa is just across the valley and he had the
Mortimers staying who introduced us to Teddy Millington-Drake so
amusing he asked us over for a drink to meet Germaine Greer who's
absolutely charming and Mark Boxer dropped in who was renting
Alexander's place he's in charge of the whole of Conde Nast now it's so
peaceful at this time of year there's just no one about ..."

"... it's not in any guide it's north of Leeds quite difficult to find just off the B3053 but once you get there it's worth every penny it's run by this couple he had that restaurant in Battersea the *Deux Poissons* you remember his wife's a model she's an American and knows all about interior design they've done it up beautifully everything's period real log fire in the lounge they make their own marmalade which shows their attention to detail it's like being in a country house as a guest you're made to feel one of the family and the food is sensational Jean-Paul chooses the wine himself direct from France and we had a '49 Latour out of this world and if you want there's fishing in the reservoir and horseriding and country walks we didn't actually do any of them it's incredibly expensive but you have to pay for quality my wife loves gardening and there's a wonderful herb garden in this huge Victorian conservatory with kiwi fruit and the views are amazing of course the air base is a bit noisy but it is half a mile away ..."

"... I'd love to go but the tickets are changing hands for thousands of pounds it's incredible mind you it's probably worth it to see that level of play did you watch the Welsh game amazing to see them getting stuffed at home first time in how many years was it? the England pack were amazing and we haven't seen running like that from the backs since well I don't know that Rory Underwood try was unbelievable the Scots will have to be pretty sharp to stop our lads when they're on this sort of form I put it down to the Lions tour Rob Andrew has really come on no I think we're talking Grand Slam here Bill Beaumont was saying that they're a better side than his lot and I agree with that their sheer fitness is staggering and when you combine that with their handling skills and their dominance in the ruck well it's dynamite I'd love to go but you get a much better picture on the box ..."

"... it's better than *The Fly* any day there's a great bit in it when his whole face explodes and all this pus comes out and then this bird who's with him starts turning green and all these worms come out of her eyes it's fantastic I dunno how they do it have you seen the one where all the zombies come up from the grayeyard and you can see all their flesh falling off and this huge maggot crawls out of one of them's ear and eats the dog by dissolving it in slime I tell you it was magic I nearly threw up and my girlfriend had nightmares for months I hear there's a new one in the States which no one is allowed to see where this man gives birth to a giant cockroach which eats him and lives off nuclear waste apparently at the preview most of the audience died of shock it should be out over here soon ..."

"... the market's gone crazy I mean did you read about the cupboard in Knightsbridge which went for $95,000 and yet last week we were up in Cumberland seeing Penny's mother and we saw this amazing old priory which has been converted into a hotel it's got 18 rooms, 29 acres, stables and outbuildings and a small cottage in the grounds and it's going for 12 grand you could probably get it for less if you give them cash have you seen the latest copy of *Country Life* it's incredible what you can pick up Grade One listed buildings, Georgian stately homes, landscape gardens all for half the price of a garage up here I mean I can easily fax my stuff in and there's an airport in Huddersfield which apparently does a shuttle I mean we're seriously thinking about moving out and you've got to get in fast Gloucestershire's peaked already it's the same story in Dorset if you want to make big money I'd start buying up the border country before it goes the same way we saw a castle going for 3 grand ... "

". . . I am afraid I really can't make any comment at this stage I'm
sorry gentlemen I have nothing to say to you at this moment in time no
I'm sorry at a later stage I may be able to oblige you but as of now I have
nothing to add as you know my previous statement thankyou thankyou
thankyou very much I'm sure you must have more interesting things to
do excuse me what was that no I repeat what I have already said to you
that I can say absolutely nothing to you I'm sure we're all very tired and
its been a very long day I appreciate the fact that you're only doing your
job but I have my job to do and as I said earlier it would not appropriate
for me to make any comment at this stage I'm sorry gentlemen . . ."

". . . you may think 28 stone is a lot but when you see them they're so graceful two men locked in physical combat I don't understand the rules myself but it's an art form really of enormous subtlety it goes back thousands of years to samurai warriors they have a special diet of beanshoots and raw fish which makes them incredibly heavy and that's all they do their whole life it's like a religion actually well it is a religion they are not wrestlers more like priests they have all these rituals with the water which I don't understand but it's incredibly artistic it's not really sport I've always wanted to go to Japan fascinating place apparently they have no street names and the houses are made of paper because of the earthquakes we think of them as barbaric but actually when you see these men it's exactly like ballet . . ."

"... it was wonderful to get away we were absolutely in the middle of nowhere no noise no traffic and no telly it's an old schoolhouse with this tremendous old stove that's been there for yonks you just look out the window and there are all these sheep it's so peaceful the children just love it you know we go for really long walks and you don't have to lock up because everyone's so friendly and the local shops are just unbelievable I mean proper bread and fresh vegetables it's so cheap and there's a woman in the village who does just everything and she makes a fuss when you give her a fiver it's so embarrassing door to door it's hardly three hours and it's another world anyway what's been happening while we were away I'm dying to know ..."

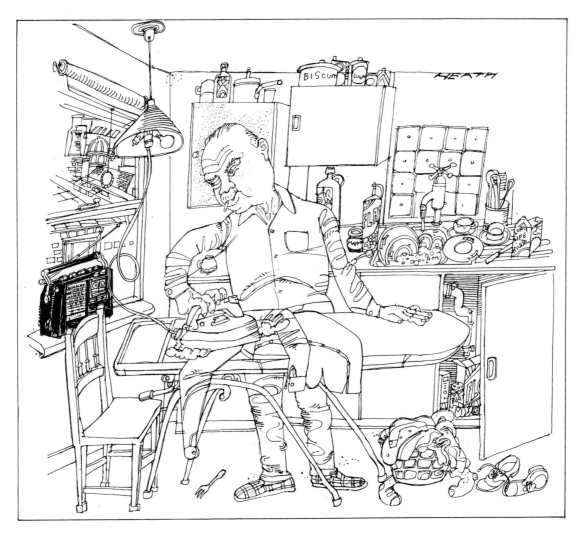

"... I agree with Robert what is so maddening is that the man in front of
you at the checkout counter wears socks made of fablon or nulon and you
know that he's the sort of chap who has double glazing in his bathroom
nothing wrong with that of course you may say we all at one time or another
have tried to grab the soap on the rope in the shower and missed ha ha ha
almost as if that man in front of you in the slow lane of the motorway of life
has bought that Volvo just to annoy you ha ha ha and now Instant Sunshine
toot their horn in our direction as it were ... we've got double glazing we've
got double glazing in our swedish Volvo car we've got double glazing we've
... thank you Instant Sunshine how do they do it Ann anything you can offer
us ever so humble though it be which brings to mind toothpowder or is it in
the tube you squeeze at one end or in my case in the middle? ha ha ha many a
marriage has gone bust on less Ann? ... well you may well ask I was in
China nothing wrong with China per se but they don't have toilet paper ...
ha ha ha oh come come Ann no it's true anyway the hotel I was in ..."

"... amazing when you think about it 38 billion miles away and only two seconds late in Neptune and it's powered by a battery 20 million times weaker than an ordinary watch battery and it's still sending back perfect pictures did you see those volcanoes on one of those moons apparently it's the one that goes round anti-clockwise which is impossible and it's night for 58 years and a million degrees below zero yet this thing's still working perfectly and it's going to go on into space for ever you'd have thought with that kind of technology you could make a phone call to Reading and why can't British Rail get a train to run on time bloody amazing really it's 12 years old tell me who's driving a car that's 12 years old look at light bulbs three weeks maximum in our house it's not as if they were cheap ..."

". . . Afrika Afrika riffin' boo yaa yo yo ice-t hip hop rap rap warrior warri warri awesome chillin' fly chillin' fly awesome boo yaa don't let peer pressure get you down Flash Master def happenin' happenin' happenin' happenin' riot in Lagos blaster doin' it Ka$h da Masta phase four funki ziphood ziphood sparks for the kids street slam yo lo-top MC Duke rap warrior boo yaa don't quit wreckin' crew outlaw posse posse future kool kulture skool awesome baad speak on reality boo yo thank you very much good night . . ."

# ET CETERA

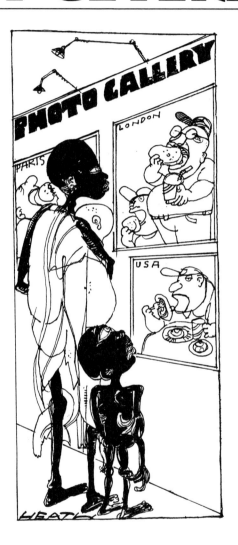

from *The Independent* and *The Spectator*

'. . . I was evacuated to this village in 1940.
I just came back to see how it was.'

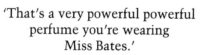
'That's a very powerful powerful
perfume you're wearing
Miss Bates.'

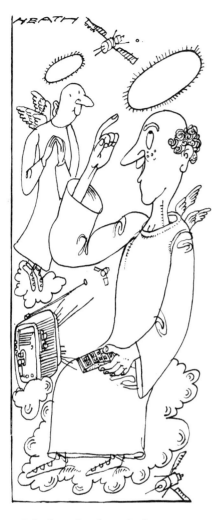

'I find with a bit of adjustment
I can pick up all the channels.'

'Doctors advised sea air.'

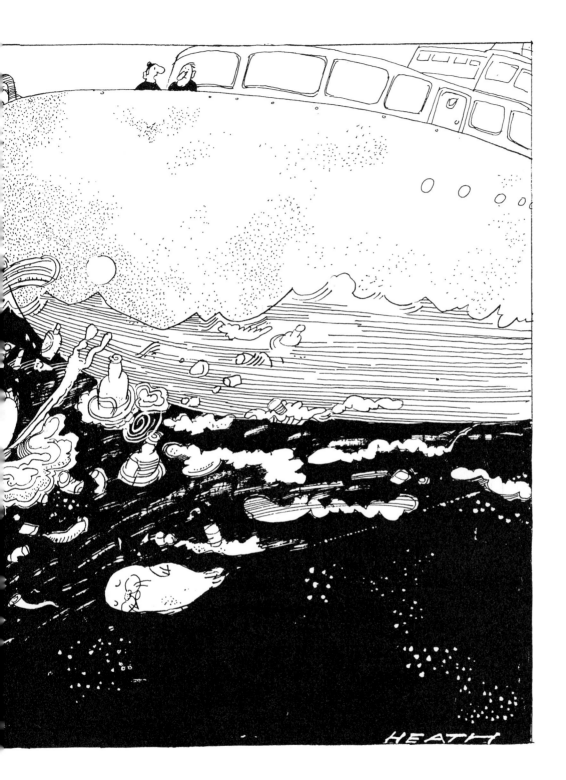

'They're dying like flies, but nobody knows why.'

'Careful sir! It's the critics!'

'He's great! I wonder who
his PR is'

'It's a repeat!'

Inner city deprivation.

'Dear, oh dear, you see the next play we've got coming up for you! Sex, perversions, you name it, it's got the lot!'

'What is a heterosexual?'

A page from Mrs Thatcher's sketchbook.

'I put it to you that you are a Nazi war criminal!'

'Order in Court.'

'Bleedin' typical! Whenever you want
one there's never one around!'

'OK, so they call me crazy,
so I'll end up in Carey St,
but I'm not asking £60m . . .
I'm not asking £55m . . .'

'It's the only place
that's not open on a Sunday.'

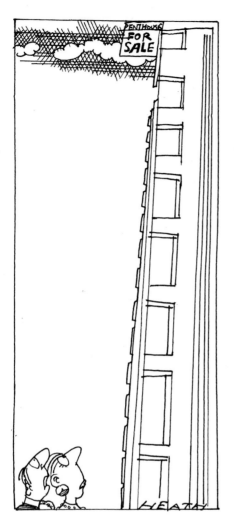

'He couldn't afford the
repayments so he jumped.'

'It's allright officer, I'm not an anarchist,
I'm a property developer.'